in-line skater's start-up

a beginner's guide to in-line skating and roller hockey

The
Start-Up Sports
Series, #4

By Doug Werner

Published By
Tracks Publishing
San Diego, California

In-Line Skater's Start-Up

A Beginner's Guide to In-Line Skating and Roller Hockey

By Doug Werner

Published by:
Tracks Publishing
140 Brightwood Avenue
Chula Vista, CA 91910
(619) 476-7125 Fax (619) 476-8173

All rights reserved. No part of this book may be reproduced or transmitted in any form or by any means, electronic or mechanical, including photocopying, recording or by any information storage and retrieval system without written permission from the author, except for the inclusion of brief quotations in a review.

Copyright © 1995 by Doug Werner
Second Printing 1996

Publisher's Cataloging in Publication
(Prepared by Quality Books Inc.)

Werner, Doug, 1950-
   In-Line skater's start-up : a beginner's guide to in-line skating and roller hockey / Doug Werner.
   p. cm. – (Start-up sports)
   Includes bibliographical references and index.
   Preassigned LCCN: 95-60153
   ISBN: 1-884654-04-5

   1. In-line skating. I. Title. II. Series.

GV859.73.W47 1995   796.21
                             QBI95-20048

Dedicated to
Christopher J. Reinhard

Acknowledgements

Kathleen Wheeler
Karhu USA, Inc.
Doug Barbor
Dave Smallwood
Don Thomson
Robin Racine
University Of San Diego
Mike Womack
Todd Melton
National In-Line Hockey Association
Joseph Mireault
Shawn Jones
Berri Goldfarb
USA Hockey InLine
Mark Rudolph
International In-Line Skating Association
Henry Zuver
Paul Chapey
American Youth Sports Foundation
Jim Schmedding
InLine Magazine
Natalie Kurylko
Kensington Type
Tamara Parsons
Play It Again Sports
Tye Smith
Kyle Schetgen
Randy Grubbs
Karin Osgood
Griffin Reinhard
Maureen Reinhard
Diane Gallo
Rudy Southerland
Fred
Bob Glassberg
Independent Publishers Group
Mark Suchomel
Bookcrafters
Cheryl Haab
Lynn's Photo
Marlo Cormier

Contents

The Skating Part 7
Intro/ *Flying Feets* 9
Chapter 1/ *Gear* 15
Chapter 2/ *Safety* 23
Chapter 3/ *Rolling Along* 27
Chapter 4/ *Stop!!* 33
Chapter 4 1/2/ *Fall from Grace* 41
Chapter 5/ *Turning* 47
Chapter 6/ *Goin' Backwards* 51
Chapter 7/ *Transitions* 57

The Hockey Part 61
Intro/ *The New Game in the Streets* 63
Chapter 8/ *Hockey Gear* 69
Chapter 9/ *The Game* 77
Chapter 10/ *Hockey Skating Skills* 81
Chapter 11/ *On the Stick* 93
Chapter 12/ *Passing* 99
Chapter 13/ *Shooting* 111
Chapter 14/ *Defensive Stick Skills* 119
Chapter 15/ *The Goalie* 125
Chapter 16/ *Playing the Game* 135

Glossary 139
Resources 145
Bibliography 149
Index 151

Special Note
Please note that on pages 30, 32, and 49 the skater is not wearing wristguards. Those pictures are in no way meant to condone skating without wristguards.

the skating part

flying feets

introduction

PLODDER NATION

Moving around on our feet is something we pretty much take for granted. Walking. Running. Skipping. Jumping. It's all a matter of lifting or springing with a leg or two.

This is also our daily struggle with gravity. The one we lose every darn day whenever we take that step, stride, or leap. For no matter who you are– butcher, baker, professional basketball player– you can only go so far before you land and have to start all over again.

We're a nation of plodders. Our natural state is stationary. If ya don't push, you're planted. Maybe couch potatoes are on to something.

But probably NOT.

Let's see. If we can't defy Mr. G....

Maybe we could just deceive the burdensome fellow a bit...

and put wheels on our feet!

WHOA!

The whole deal with this skating business can be read on the face of any beginner who has just wobbled onto their wheels for the first time.

At first the look on their face is somewhere between frustration and fear. Well, maybe terror is a better word. *OhmygodwhatamIdoingthisfor!!*

And then they start rolling. *Whoa!*

They try a shakey little stride. And then another. They roll a bit. *And away they go.*

Now! Look at their face.

Even the most hardened among us cannot hide a big pie-faced grin. Lookit ME! *I'm SKATING!*

It feels like breaking free.

And it is. It's also a wonderful feeling. A little scary, yeah, but all the same, a wonderful, **exhilarating** feeling. Because you're no longer groveling to gravity. You're rolling on top of it. And the rolling feels like flying!

It's **FUN**, in other words.

A WARNING

Ranking psychologists, shamen, and gym teachers the world over agree:

In-line skating is a pursuit that transforms the inner workings of the mind and soul to such a degree that everyday concerns such as homework, grocery shopping, lawn mowing, taxes, and spousal complaints are forgotten. Only the immediate sensations of slicing through the air on silent, spinning wheels remain on the brain.

The clinical name for this phenomena is ***kidstuff.***

There are numerous treatments for the *kidstuff syndrome* which include self-doubt, the work ethic, and propriety. However, most of these cures have dire side effects, which include weight gain, alcoholism, chronic sourpuss, and dowdiness. For these reasons a growing number of *kidstuff* specialists tend to think it best to just let the afflicted skate.

Dr. Timothy Schmitt of Bunkum University has recently completed a 5-year study of the *kidstuff syndrome* as it relates to in-line skating. He is acknowledged by many to be the leading expert in the field. Schmitt's findings are particularly significant to those about to try the sport.

"After years of careful observation, it is my opinion that the entire lot of them [in-line skaters] are acting like a bunch of damn kids. Even the ones old enough to know better. Imagine if we all acted that way. Boy, oh, boy! What a sorry state of affairs that would be."

There it is.

FITNESS

We've got more studies. This one's from the University of Massachusetts:

"In-line skating at moderate speeds or faster burns as many calories as running."

Here's mine:

In-line skating is a terrific workout. You don't bang or twist your joints when you do it. Unless you skate into a tree.

You can get a workout equal to running if you travel at least twice as far.

It isn't boring unless you're skating against a strong wind. But then it's a better workout that way.

Actually, it's less a workout and more a recreation that's good for you.

IT'S A RAGE

In case you haven't noticed, in-line skaters are everywhere. There are over 15 million across the USA and that was the last time I checked. It's an activity that literally everyone does. Rich, poor, fat, skinny, young, old, boy, girl, man, woman... everybody.

Like playing the guitar, **it's relatively easy to pick up and enjoy right away**, yet you can evolve with it, too, and make it as challenging as you want it to be.

It's relatively inexpensive and all you need is a sidewalk.

Although it may look a little scary to some, **it's only as risky as you make it.**

As stated earlier, **it's a fun way to be active and keep fit.**

For these reasons and others, in-line skating has taken off in the past 5-10 years big time. And I thought it was something of a fad back in 1980!

Whatever happened to roller skates, anyway?

A SCHIZOIDAL APPROACH

This book has two parts. *The Skating Part* and *The Hockey Part.*

The *Skating Part* is for everyone starting out. It takes beginning matters very slow and easy. I like to explain stuff the way I wish people would explain things to me. Like I'm two clicks from brain dead.

The *Hockey Part* is for folks interested in the game as players, or parents of players, or just plain watchers.

By the way, you don't have to be a well-rounded athlete to play this game. You just need the equipment, which isn't all that much, and some friends to play with. Of course, that may be a problem for some of you.

Believe it or not, I've seen all kinds racing around with a stick. Little girls, old men. Fit, not-so-fit. Good skaters, lousy skaters. It must have something to do with all the charging and club waving. Something primeval.

Anyway, so I have these two parts that really don't connect for some of you. So you folks just read half. But you hockey types gotta read both.

I left out racing, figure skating, and extreme skating just because.

I mean, I'm not interested in giant skates, or ballroom antics, or jumping off buildings. This book was getting long enough as it was. I do have a resource section in the back, however, that'll point you in the right direction.

NO SABE

Reading about doing this stuff is not going to cut it all the time. That's why there's so many pictures. In fact, you can pick up most of the pointers in this book by gazing at the photos and reading the captions. Actually, it's better to watch the experts do it and mimic them. Because ink on paper just can't communicate, say, a backwards crossover worth a hoot.

But this book's a good running start. And it'll serve as a resource as you learn. You can even take it with you. Besides a book is always patient and always friendly, no matter how you goof up!

THIS IS THE POINT

Like all my *Start-Up Books*, this is a how-to book as seen through the eyes of a professional beginner: me.

Although I always gain proficiency, I never quite shake the humiliation and anguish of my first days as a kook. It stays with me. So I can forever relate to bumbling idiots everywhere.

But that's a bit maudlin. And less than half the story.

Because I also remember the sheer joy of finally getting it *right*.

The thrill of attaining a new athletic skill with the ability to exploit it at will is one of the *Great Sweetspots* in Life.

Anyway, doing this stuff beats most anything else that comes to mind. And more often than not, it's as good as it gets.
Enjoy yourself.

Hey, Coach. Where's <u>your</u> helmet?

THE SKATES

Rent first.

There's a million and a half makes and models from which to choose costing anywhere from $80 to $400. **Before you deal with the shop-and-buy headache, try the sport on for size for itself, all by itself. Get out there and roll!**

It should be easy to find a pair of rentals. Just check the yellow pages. Expect to pay around $4 an hour, $10 a day. The shop will want a credit card or lotsa cash.

Bring a pair of athletic socks. Argyles or nylon hose won't work.

Very small feet will end up in 3 wheelers. Most skaters use 4 wheelers. The models with 5 wheels are for racing, and that you're not going to do, yet.

THE FIT

Tell the friendly skate shop person your size and

Gear

commence to trying on skates. They should fit snugly with toes close or just brushing the toe of the boot. Loose skates won't provide enough support, and tight skates will kill you. Make sure all buckles, laces, wheels, and nuts are there and intact.

Stand up and walk/roll around the sales floor. The first thing you'll notice on quality, good fitting skates is the support. Most beginners think balancing on a single line of wheels will be difficult. Not true. From knees to wheels you're as rigid as can be. Solid and straight. No wobbly ankles.

If the skates do not provide this rigid support there's something wrong with them. Ask for another pair.

As you stumble about, keep your knees bent and concentrate on keeping your body over your feet/wheels. It might be scary at first but with a little focus and no sudden moves you'll be fine. Really. Don't let your mind run away with the slippery fears you're feeling. Good skates are made to support you.

Now is the time to determine if the fit is good. If in doubt, keep trying on skates. You will have no success out on the pavement in a poor fit. If it feels funny in the store, you'll agonize on the asphalt.

BUYING SKATES

As confusing as the selection might be, what you should look for in a skate is simple. **Good materials, solid construction, and breathability are all found in the name brands. Avoid the bargain bins.** They're dirt-cheap for a reason. The respected manufacturers each offer a wide variety of quality product, and somewhere in the mix there's an affordable pair of skates made for you.

Discuss with your salesperson what your skating needs and goals are. Some weekend rolling here and

Chapter One

A good fitting pair of quality skates should be a pleasure to wear. **Buy a name brand and go for the fit.**

Note the ankle strap for extra support.

Most beginners are concerned about support in their in-line skates. Aren't they awfully wobbly? How can you balance on a single row of wheels?

In a quality pair of skates it's just not a problem!

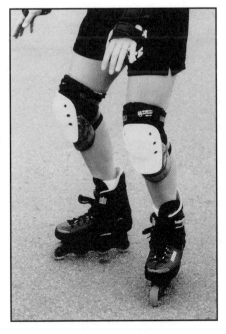

Gear

Geared up and ready to roll! *From head to toe: helmet, elbow pads, wrist guards, and knee pads. It's not alot to wear, the good stuff is light, and it doesn't impede your skating.*

there? Regular fitness training? Serious sport? Transportation? Chances are (s)he will be quite helpful since most folks who work in skate shops are skaters anyway and pretty much in the know.

Once you've narrowed down the selection in this fashion start trying on the skates you can afford. Buckles, space-age design, and the latest brake system are convenient/cool but not essential. A hinged cuff is a very good idea and incorporated into most of the new skates. The cuff is the top of the boot. The hinge allows for flexibility when you bend your knees, which is proper skating posture anyway.

As you shop you'll encounter some other skate features that may or may not be issues when you make your selection. Not all wheels are the same. They come in a variety of diameters, degrees of hardness, widths, and core types. Bearings can be grease or oil, and may even have a precision rating. There are shells and inner-boots and frames to consider as well.

Yes, it can get confusing, but many of these concerns are for more experienced skaters. And depending on what use you have in mind for your skates, all these factors have already been resolved for you. So decide how you wanna skate, choose from the appropriate category, and pick a pair that best fits your budget and feet.

When in doubt, GO FOR THE FIT!

MORE ABOUT WHEELS

And more than you need to know for now!

DIAMETER

Wheels range in size from 64mm to 80mm. Larger wheels are faster in racing conditions. However, smaller wheels accelerate more quickly.

PROFILE

This is the thickness of the wheel. The widest wheels

are made for hockey and provide the best cornering. The thinner you go, the faster you go. Thinner wheels are less stable and wear out sooner than fatter ones.

DUROMETER

This is the hardness of the wheel. The durometer can range from 74A to 92A and higher. Softer wheels have a higher grip on any surface and provide a smoother ride than harder wheels, but wear out faster. Harder wheels are faster on smooth surfaces.

CORE

This is the hub of the wheel that surrounds the bearings. Cores come open with spokes or holes, or closed and solid. Open cored wheels are lighter and faster than those with closed cores. Closed cored wheels last longer than open cored wheels because you can wear them down farther.

MORE ABOUT BEARINGS

Just in case you wanna know.

Cheap and/or beginner skates have no rating. More advanced skates have an ABEC-1, -3, or -5 rating. The higher the rating, the faster you go. Oil bearings are initially faster than grease bearings and require more maintenance than grease bearings.

ROCKERING

Brand new skates come out of the box with all wheels in a straight line, level to each other. Some models can be rockered by lowering the middle wheel(s) or by placing smaller wheels in the front and rear slots.

Rockering enables the more advanced skater to pivot and turn tighter. Hockey players in particular like to rocker their skates in order to increase maneuverability. Tools to adjust the frame spacers on your skate should come with your purchase.

MAINTENANCE

Rotating and Turning the Wheels

The wheels on your skates will wear sooner on their inside edge and become lopsided over time. The inside edges of the wheels (the skater's instep) do all the pushing, stopping, and dragging. Hence the need to periodically rotate and turn the wheels as shown.

Other than, that just keep your skates clean and periodically check wheels for tightness. Bearings should last through several wheel changes. Replace the brake when it wears down.

PROTECTION

The last time I checked, asphalt and cement were still hard. Injuries related to in-line skating always seem to be running at an all time high. You don't have to get hurt doing this skating stuff. **Skate wisely and cautiously, and wear the proper protective gear.**

HELMET

It seems a bit much until you've dealt with your first noggin rebound! All kidding aside, this is an important precaution. Most especially for the pee-wees. Make `em wear one.

WRIST GUARDS

An absolute must since the first thing that usually hits the pavement in a fall is your hand. Wrist guards provide a hard plastic support that absorbs the shock and protects the rather complicated and otherwise vulnerable arrangement of bones in the wrist.

KNEE AND ELBOW PADS

Check out some used pads sometime. Imagine those scrapes on your body!

Gear

Rotating the wheels-- *This illustration shows the proper rotation for a four-wheel skate. If skates only have three wheels, the front wheel rotates to the rear and the others move forward by one slot.*

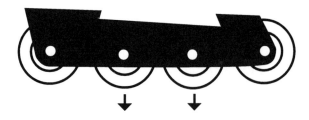

Rockering the wheels-- *On skates that allow it, the middle wheels are slotted lower than the end ones. This allows only two wheels to ride the surface at any given time, thus increasing maneuverability. The same effect can be obtained by inserting smaller wheels in the front and rear slots.*

safety/ 2

The International In-Line Skating Association (IISA) has it wired:

RULES OF THE ROAD

1) Wear protective gear including helmet, knee and elbow pads, and wrist guards.
2) Achieve a basic skating level before taking to the road.
3) Stay alert and be courteous at all times.
4) Always skate under control.
5) Skate on the right side of paths, trails, and sidewalks.
6) Overtake pedestrians, cyclists, and other skaters on the left.
7) Stay away from water, oil, and debris on the trail, and uneven or broken pavement.
8) Observe all traffic regulations.
9) Avoid areas with heavy automotive traffic.
10) Always yield to pedestrians.

Safety

Not a good place to skate. Although so many skaters wind up in places like this. It's crowded, wet, and narrow.

Where ya gonna land if you crash and burn?

Much, much better! No crowd, the surface is smooth, and *there's lots of turf for tumbling.*

Chapter Two

AT LEAST REMEMBER THIS

Safety is always an exercise in common sense. Until you can really do it, skate on flat, smooth areas away from everybody and everything.

Always wear your protective gear, avoid your local suicide hill, **always wear your protective gear**, when in doubt slow down, **always wear your protective gear**, don't hitch rides behind cars, **always wear your protective gear**, and stay off the interstate.

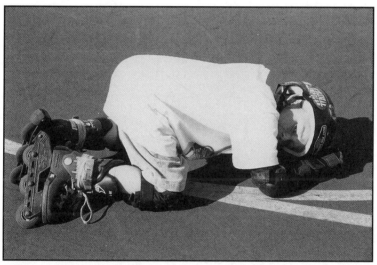

Hey no big deal! *He's geared for the big fall.*

Safety

You're not gonna run into a mailbox if you're aware of your surroundings. Keep your head up and your eyes peeled like this guy. **Don't stare at your skates!**

rolling along/3

Smooth, flat, and desolate is a perfect description of the ideal Beginnerville. Tennis courts, strandways, wide/straight sidewalks, and parking lots are good bets. Avoid cracked, pot-holed, gravelly, oily, coarse, and/or poorly patched surfaces. You don't need tons of room, but you do need some. The guy/gal who rented/sold you your skates should know where you can flail most safely around town. So ask!

THE STANCE

OK. You got the skates and you got the place. Sit down and put on your wheels. Carefully stand, and **assume a bent-kneed crouch/stance.** Feet are shoulder width. Hands are held out in front. Keep your weight over the wheels. **This is the skater's stance.**

Until you have gained a whole lot more confidence and proficiency than you now have, **do not stand up straight on your skates.** It's much too easy for your

Rolling Along

Skater's Stance-- *Check it out. Skates are shoulder width. Knees are bent and the skater assumes a slight crouch. Weight is always over the wheels.* **The skates won't slip away when you're centered and balanced like this.**

weight to settle on the heels. As soon as that happens you'll be on your back.

Concentrate! Think of the skates as extensions of your feet. That they really do belong there. And that you belong on top of them. If you feel wobbly, hold on to something upright or have a pal steady you.

NO FEAR

If you have never roller skated, or ice skated, skateboarded, skied, or surfed, it's gonna feel strange. Ah heck. It'll feel strange no matter what! Rolling just ain't natural.

But that doesn't mean it has to be scary. If you're feeling real insecure, have your pal just push you along for a bit so you can get used to that rollin' feelin'. Keep yourself in the skater's stance with your weight over the wheels.

See. It's a snap!

TIME FOR YOUR SOLO: *STRIDENGLIDE*

In the skater's stance, sorta turn your feet out a bit. Like a duck. Push off on one foot, stride and glide *(stridenglide!)* ahead with the other, push off on that foot, stride and glide with the other, and so on. **Don't walk!** Use little baby *stridenglides* at first to get the idea. **Keep yourself over the wheels!**

Maintain the *stridenglide*. Pushing off to the side with one foot, and striding and gliding with the other. **It's this pushing-off-to-the-side stuff that propels you. Just sliding the skates along in a shuffle doesn't work.**

RHYTHM

Skating along in a smooth, comfortable, and efficient fashion is a rhythm thing. It takes a little time and practice to get it down. Like learning a new dance step. The

Rolling Along

Stroke *(left to right)*-- Each leg and skate takes a turn pushing off to the side using the entire row of wheels until the leg is straight. The leg returns underneath the hips with knee bent to steer and support while the other side strokes. Note the shifts in weight. *(See page 6.)*

knack of pushing and striding along on wheels will come sooner for some, later for others. Watch the other skaters who do it well. Look at their motion. Get a feel for the rhythm.

When you're doing it right, it feels right. Like hitting a tennis ball. When *ya gots the rhythm*, you're not fighting it. At first your feet or ankles may ache. Maybe your back. That's because it's awkward and you're battling with your body parts.

Believe in this:

That rolling along can be as natural and comfy as walking or running. There is a way! And of course, you can do it!

WEIGHT/UNWEIGHT

As you first stride and push, many of you will never really want to shift your weight from pushing skate to striding skate, to pushing skate to striding skate, etc. It just seems too scary to allow one foot the responsibility to carry most of the weight. Even for a nano-second. So you end up doing this shuffling thing where each skate never really pushes much or strides much.

This is clumsy and totally defeats what skating is all about: *the seemingly effortless and rhythmic gliding of feet-on-wheels over pavement.*

If you find yourself doing this clip-clopping, hold it right there and watch the experts do it. Look at the pix alongside this text. Note the to-and-fro, the weight/unweight, the **gracefulness** that comes with proper stroking.

Eventually you must trust yourself to shift your weight from one skate to the other. That's what will give you the rhythm, the motion, the technique, and eventually the smooth, flowing stroke. It'll just feel right. It'll feel good. And you won't feel achy or tired doing it.

Rolling Along

You gotta learn how to skate with confidence and control with each foot. *Each skate must be able to support and steer you for the time it takes to stroke and brake properly. (See Page 6.)*

stop!! 4

Stopping may seem tricky on in-line skates at first. Coordinating mind, body, and skates in order to achieve halting power is usually the first really difficult task for budding skaters.

That's why so many folks are skating about without knowing how to stop very well. And, in large part, why there are so many accidents.

But if people had to learn how to stop before they could circle the park with their friends, nobody would bother skating. It takes a long time to get really good at stopping.

Not that that is a good excuse to skate around like so many run-away trains, but everyone wants to get going ASAP. I mean who wants to practice stopping?

So.

At this point in your putt-putting around, stay away from hills and other skaters. Make sure your skating areas are roomy enough to glide to a halt. Don't go so

Stop!

fast that you cannot slow down and stop without running into something or someone. If possible, learn right next to a grassy area so that if the worse thing happens, you can tumble onto some turf.

The trick to the basic stopping methods is learning how to balance on one skate. You need to be able to shift and balance most of your weight on the one braking skate and still control your skating.

This is what takes time to learn. You're not going to get it right away. For most folks it's just too awkward and scary.

So take it a bit at a time. As you skate each day. Practice the basic stopping methods (that are coming up) going very slowly at first. Over the course of time you'll get it.

BUT MEANWHILE learn some slowing techniques so that you can get out there and have some control. As long as you skate in *Beginnerville* (smooth, flat, and desolate) that oughta be enough to ensure a modicum of safety.

SLOWING TECHNIQUES

THE OL' IN AND OUT

As you glide, point your toes out and in, out and in, so that your legs splay and come together again repetitively. This will cut down on your forward momentum.

SNOWPLOW

From a glide, point your toes in slightly and let the line of wheels on each skate rub sideways for a moment along the pavement. Push down and out on your skates so that the inside (instep side) of the wheels rub the pavement. Don't hold the **V** of the snowplow for long. Sorta go in and out of it in a rocking fashion. If you hold the snowplow for too long, your feet will crash into each other and bad things could happen.

Chapter Four

The Ol' In and Out *(left to right)-- A simple way to slow down. From a glide just point your skates way out, and in. Way out, and in. This slows your forward momentum.*

Stop!

Snowplow – *From a glide go into The Ol' In and Out. As your skates begin to come together, dig the inside edges of your wheels into the pavement. Don't let your skates run into each other. If you don't stop all the way during a cycle, point out and try again.*

Chapter Four

Turn Stop *(left to right)– From a glide separate the legs and put your weight on one skate. Let it turn you around. The other skate acts as a pivot.*

TURN STOP

We're getting a little ahead of ourselves here, but so what. Turning in a glide will impede your forward motion and slow you down.

From a glide position, splay your skates slightly so that your legs begin to separate. As they do, put pressure on one skate and make it turn you around. Look and lean into the direction you're going. To go right, let the left foot turn you. To go left, let the right foot turn you. The other foot should just tag along and act as a pivot as you turn around.

BASIC STOPS

WEIGHT/UNWEIGHT (AGAIN!)

Before you get into the basic stopping techniques, learn how to skate and balance on one skate by simply weighting and unweighting. That is, as you practice the basic stroke and glide, linger on one skate a tad longer than usual. This will force you to balance all your weight on one set of wheels.

When you feel wobbly, just unweight and stroke with the other foot. Keep it up until you feel more and more comfy doing this flamingo impression.

It's really important to get good at this or stopping and lotsa other stuff just won't happen.

USING THE HEEL BRAKE

Your skates will probably have a heel brake on the right skate. It can be removed and bolted onto the other skate if it feels better there.

The basic heel brake is just a rubber stop that works when you tilt the toe of your foot up and drag the rubber along the pavement.

In a glide, crouch down, push the brake skate ahead of the other, align it with the the other skate's rear wheel, and tilt the brake skate up. With your hands out in front, slow down and stop.

Chapter Four

Heel Brake-- *Making it look easy. In order to stop with the heel brake you gotta be able to balance on one skate. It takes some practice to get the knack.*

T-Stop-- *The braking skate must be at a right angle to the forward skate which points straight ahead. The trick is applying just the right amount of pressure to the dragging skate's wheels.*

*The **toe-stop** is very similar. Instead of dragging the entire line of wheels, however, only the front wheel is used.*

Stop!

Much easier said than done. Just practice doing it slowly. Get a feel for body position as you crouch, bend at the knees, and brake.

Now you might have a pair of skates that boast a more modern, user-friendly braking system than the one described. Although the braking function may be easier to perform, chances are it still involves rubbing a heel brake on the pavement with one foot. That means you still must develop a sense of balance while braking with one skate. You're not going to get away from that unless you carry around some dorky, rake-like device in your hands and drag it behind you. (Yes, they do make such things. And NO!, it's not a viable alternative. It impedes your arm stroke and it looks like an old Three Stooges prop.)

T-STOP

This somewhat more advanced stopping technique involves dragging the wheels of one skate at right angles behind the other. What makes this method such a bear is the tendency for the braking skate to spin you. The trick is to apply just the right amount of downward pressure on your braking wheels while maintaining a perfect **T** position with your skates.

TOE-STOP

This is a bit easier than the full-on T-stop. Instead of dragging all the wheels of your braking skate, just use the front or toe wheel of the braking skate.

fall from grace/4 1/2

IF HE'D ONLY WORN A HELMET

You're gonna fall.

Sometimes you can do something about it and sometimes you can't. For those times you can't, you'll soon develop a very deep and meaningful relationship with your protective gear. Oft times all that lies between your precious parts and true pain (or much worse) is some plastic. **Wear your stuff!**

DON'T STAND UP!

Before many a topple, especially in the beginning, you can feel it coming. That cozy, secure feeling of balance and weight over the wheels just sorta drifts away. For a long second or two it's like gliding on air. Maybe you ran into a pebble. Or one of your skates lost an edge. Maybe another skater brushed by you and caught you unawares. Or maybe you're only psyching yourself out.

It doesn't matter. What you've become is tipsy. You're

Fall From Grace

*When ya feel it slippin' away, **don't stand up!** This is every beginner's first reaction to any imbalance.*

Your weight goes right to your heels and your skates will immediately squirt out ahead.

*If you feel a fall coming on, bend your knees and **lower your center of gravity.** This'll stabilize you and prevent the most heinous of skating mishaps: the Butt Slam. (Which quite often brings on a Skull Bounce. And that's serious stuff, indeed.)*

at that stage when the eyes get real big and the moaning starts. Some folks go into a trance and some folks get to hollering. Everyone has an interesting and unique way to prepare for a crash.

However there is one thing all tipsy-to-tumble (T&T) crashes have in common (not to be confused with out-of-the-blue (OB) calamities such as rocketing skateboarders, car doors, or meteor showers). **In all T&T mishaps, just before the crash itself, the tipsy skater stands ramrod straight and begins waving at the sky.**

Don't do that.

When ya feel it slippin' away:
1) **Don't panic.**
2) **Bend at the knees and crouch.** Of course, you should already be bent and crouched somewhat if you're in the skater's stance. Just get lower.
3) **Concentrate on recovery**. Chanting *Holy-cow-I'm-gonna-fall* over and over at this point will most certainly guarantee disaster.

Why do people like to stand up when they lose their balance? Science hasn't an answer. It's like a reflex or something.

Unfortunately, it's a very bad one. For **as soon as you stand up on moving skates your weight goes to your heels. From there it's a very short trip to Buttbreak Falls.**

HOLYCOWI*REALLY*AMFALLING

If you can't regain control, at least you're in an excellent position to tuck and roll. **Just grab your knees and roll with it.** Again, the main thing is to avoid having your skates sweep out from under you. Besides

Fall From Grace

Taking a Tumble *(clockwise)-- Get low, curl up, and roll with it.*

Note the strategic use of protective gear. Falling like this without the stuff is murder.

rearranging your can, a fall like that can dent the back of your head. And that ain't funny. Believe me.

And if you can control the landing of your crash, **aim towards the softest spot around**. Like the grass next to the sidewalk. Or the sand next to the strand.

As mentioned earlier, you'd be wise to skate next to soft shoulders until you've mastered the basics of stopping and turning.

SO HOW COME THEY DON'T MAKE GIANT BUTT PADS OR SOMETHING?

Now that's a good question. I've always thought that the padding the Michelin Man wears would be terrific for in-line skating. But he never seems to be in when I've called to ask him about it.

Another winning thought would be to attach air bags fore and aft. Bump into anything and you'd blow up into a huge beach ball.

Obviously the market is wide open for new ideas. And I'm sure somebody wants to hear yours!

Fall From Grace

turning/5

SIMPLE TURNS

Turning is easier than stopping. Turning is letting the outside skate in a given turn have its own way. If you wanna go left, your outside skate will be the right one. Put your weight on it and simply lean into the turn with your shoulders. If you go right, let the left skate turn you.

Congratulations!

You now know about as much as 75% of the skating population. Enough to cruise comfortably and safely on any byway in Beginnerville. But don't stop! The rest of this stuff just makes skating even more fun.

CROSSOVERS

In order to maintain or increase speed and control during a turn, you must keep striding through it with cross-steps or crossovers. To turn right, the left skate must cross over in front of the right. To go left, the right skate must cross over in front of the left.

Turning

Simple Turn *(counterclockwise)-- Keep your knees bent and let the outside skate turn you. Just put your weight on it and lean into the direction you want to go.*

Chapter Five

Crossovers *(counterclockwise)-- As you lean into the turn, push off your inside skate. Lift and cross your outside skate over and ahead of the other. Each skate takes turns holding the edge throughout the turn.* (See page 6.)

Turning

In either case the mechanics are simple. As one skate pushes off and crosses over, the other must hold its edge until the crossing skate has planted its edge. Then the other skate pushes off. As in the simple turns, the outside skate controls the direction of the turn as well as the turn of your shoulders.

This is one of those things that can be trickier in the mind than actually doing it. **Again, you need the confidence which comes from being able to skate-your-weight on one foot.** Since as you cross over, one skate is supporting you for a split second.

Once you do it and do it right, it'll feel good, and the impossibility of doing it will fade. A phenomenon that will repeat itself with each new skating skill you attempt.

Hey! Remember it can be done!

goin' backwards / 6

Easier than you may think.

THE HOUR GLASS

Place your feet together and assume the skater's stance. Make your feet go pigeon-toed and push off. As your legs splay you should be going backwards. As the skates splay a bit wider than your shoulders, turn both heels inward, so that your legs come back together again. Repeat this in-and-out routine to continue your backwards journey.

Oh. And watch where you're going.

The hour glass is the easiest way to get going backwards. Both skates move in sync and wheels never leave the pavement.

C CUTTING

In order to gain speed and maneuverability it's necessary to develop a backwards stroke, where one skate

Goin' Backwards

Backwards Hourglass *(left to right)-- From a still position, point your toes in and push off. Let your legs splay a bit, then sweep them back towards each other. As they come together, turn your heels out again and push off.*

Chapter Six

C Cutting *(Left to right)-- Backwards push is provided by stroking motions with each skate. One after the other. Each skate pushes off and makes a **C** swipe against the pavement.*

pumps, then the other, in a side-to-side, weight/unweight, rhythmic movement.

Unlike the forward stroke, the skates hardly leave the pavement. Push off on the inside wheels of one skate and make a C cut or swipe with it. Heel out, heel in. As you complete a swipe with one foot, push off and begin a swipe with the other. Link the C cuts, develop a rhythm, and watch out for the dumpster.

Turning at this point is simply a matter of pushing off harder on one foot than the other.

BACKWARDS CROSSOVERS (NO WAY!)

The hardest thing about skating backwards is developing the crossover a-goin thatta way. It's really a different dimension at first. Going backwards and cross-stepping is against most people's sense of time and space.

The trick is that this crossover doesn't involve as much cross-stepping as the forward crossover. In fact, the skate that does the crossing never leaves the pavement.

To turn left, push off the outside edges of your left skate and sorta glide the right foot across the trail of the left, and push off the inside edge of the right skate. Then lift the left skate up and over to the start position.

It feels real wacky at first but it has its own rhythm and feel when you do it right. It's a very graceful maneuver when executed properly and a real confidence-builder to learn.

This one takes some time to master if only because it's so disorienting at first. You're gonna get dizzy for one thing so be satisfied with smaller bits of improvement over the long haul.

Chapter Six

Backwards Crossovers *(counterclockwise)-- The outside skate slides in front of the toe of the inside skate and pushes off. The other skate is then lifted alongside. The outside skate doesn't leave the pavement in all its snaking about. Note the shoulder turn in the top photos.*

Goin' Backwards

transitions
7

Making the transition from forward skating to backward skating, and visa verse, is almost impossible to write about. Almost impossible to illustrate. Heck, it looks impossible to do! But it's not so very difficult to pickup.

Basically, you pivot with one skate, swoop around with the other, and make sure both lines of wheels are headed in the right direction. It's a swift trick. You'll probably get it faster than you think. The hard(er) part comes at higher speeds. And even that is more of a mental thing.

Practice at slow speeds until you gain the knack. Make sure you keep yourself over the wheels, with knees bent, and a low center of gravity.

Other than that, just think positive. As trite as that sounds, it really is the key.

Transitions

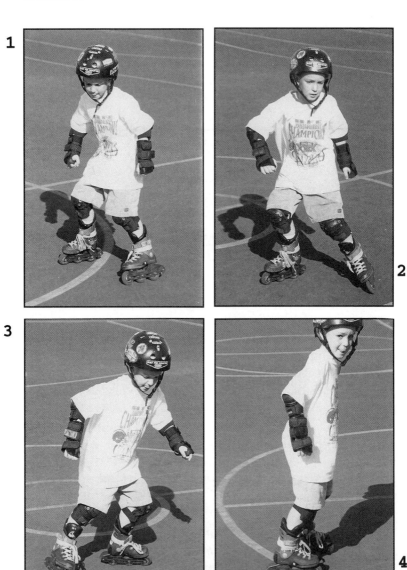

Forwards to Backwards *(left to right)-- The forward skate holds the edge while the back skate turns around 180 degrees. As soon as the back skate lands, sweep the other skate around alongside heel first.*

Chapter Seven

And Backwards to Forwards *(left to right)-- Again, one skate holds the edge while the other flips around. As soon as that skate takes the edge, the other is placed alongside.*

Transitions

the hockey part

the new game in the streets

When I was growing up we played kickball in the streets. Or some sort of baseball or football game. Little girls skated around on those metal roller skates that they strapped to their shoes. (Does anybody remember skate keys?)

Guys didn't do much skating. It was perceived to be an off-shoot of figure skating which was pretty much a girl thing as far as we were concerned. I mean Peggy Fleming was the big name in that sport. Us guys all aspired to be Sandy Koufaxes or Johnny Unitases (yes, I know I'm dating myself).

Now it's in-line skating. And in-line hockey. **There's 14 million in-line skaters across the USA and of those, over 4 million play hockey.** There's amateur leagues, professional leagues, even talk of an Olympic event. It's all over the place.

And it's popular for a very good reason:
It's a BLAST!

The first time I ever played I was just barely competent as a basic skater. I could stroke, go backwards (slowly), do transitions (very slowly), and do forward crossovers.

I played with a friend who was hell-on-wheels and his pre-kindergarten son. I tried in vain to keep up with the kid. They taught me the rudiments of puck whacking and passing, and then *it was time for a game!*

It was fast, awkward, very loose, and **way, way too much fun.**

And that's how most of you will probably learn. You won't be skating very well. You won't know anything about the game. Your ability to use the stick will be minimal. But who cares?

What's great about hockey (besides the absolute raging thrill of running amok with a curved stick) is how it improves your skating. See, you don't think about wheels when you play the game because you're trying to keep up with the action.

The learning curve for *all* the skills mentioned in the first part of this book shoots straight up without you even thinking about it.

Probably *because* you aren't thinking about it!

GET SOME INSTRUCTION

But **you can only stumble so far without coaching**. It is especially important to get an expert's advice and help with the more advanced skating and stick handling skills. In-the-flesh coaching is indispensable. And playing with more experienced players will probably be your best instruction of all.

YOU DON'T HAVE TO BE A GUY

Last week a little girl scored three goals on me in a pick-up game. Next week she's bringing her mom.

The game is fast and there's some jostling, for sure, but

it ain't ice hockey or football either. **It's a game of skill and teamwork.** The real rough stuff isn't allowed.

After saying that, please note that the use of the pronouns *he, him, himself,* etc. aren't used to exclude our female players. It's just easier to read than *he/she, him/her, himself/herself*, etc.

COME ON GRAMPS, LET'S SHOOT!

Just like so many activities in life, it's more a matter of desire than age. Heck, *I'm* 44. Pinned up at one of our local rinks is an article about some guy who's 72 and just starting out! If you wanna play, ***play***. Nobody's gonna check your ID.

HUH?

If the writing doesn't make any sense, look at the pix. If the pix don't make any sense, hire a coach and use this book for a door jam. Not all of the following skills translate to print as well as others. But in general, there's more than enough here to get you going and then some.

HAVE FUN

The FUN word keeps popping up and it is irritating, I know. It's such a lightweight word. I suppose that's why action sport jargon is replete with hipper synonyms such as *raging, epic, awesome, bitchin'*, et al. But the thing is, that's what pursuits such as roller hockey should be all about.

I personally think everything in life should be *totally outrageous* and *way cool* all the time. I'm partially devastated every morning when I read the paper and discover that the rest of the world has a different agenda. But then I suffer from a particularly serious case of the *kidstuff syndrome*.

Don't yell at your kids or be too hard on yourself when you play the game. It'll get better with time and some effort.

The **San Diego Roller Hockey Conference** has something called the **Ten Commandments for Parents of Athletic Children** that really makes sense for *everybody* if you think about it:

1) **Make sure your children know that**, win or lose, **you love them** and are not disappointed with their performance.
2) **Be realistic** about your child's physical ability.
3) Help your child **set realistic goals.**
4) **Emphasize improved performance**, not winning. Positively reinforce improved skills.
5) **Don't relive your athletic past through your child.**
6) **Provide a safe environment** for your child's training and competition. This includes the proper use of equipment and training methods.
7) **Control your own emotions** at games and events. Don't yell at other players, coaches, or officials.
8) **Be a cheerleader for your child and the other children on the team.**
9) **Respect your child's coaches.** Communicate openly with them. If you disagree with their approach, discuss it with them.
10) **Be a positive role model for your child.** Enjoy sports yourself. Set your own goals. Live a healthy lifestyle.

Say you don't have a kid? Well replace the *child* word with one that works for you. Try friend, nephew, niece, wife, girlfriend, boyfriend, or my favorite, *inner-child.*

Girls can play, too. And how! But note the extreme lack of plastic head bonnets in this pix. Not to be emulated, readers! (Nice ponytail, though.)

hockey gear/8

PROTECTION

In hockey you need stuff to protect you from flying sticks and pucks as well as the hard pavement. Although official rules prohibit checking or blocking, there's still alotta banging, chopping, flailing, and crashing going on in a heated game. And they're all heated.

Besides protection, properly fitted, quality gear provides confidence. Players who aren't afraid of getting hurt are enabled to play all out. Which is important when everyone else is playing for keeps. Which is all the time!

Purchase all of your equipment in a respected sporting goods outlet that carries the name brands. Street hockey is big news these days and every discount store has its own mickey mouse version of hockey gear. It'll cost you in comfort and protection if you buy from the bargain bins. Believe it!

HELMET

Protection all around. You're only allotted one head with the various components.

The little ones should wear a face guard. Most under-18 leagues require full face protection. It's a great idea for everybody, actually. There are two types. The plexiguard provides complete protection but can fog up. The bird-cage model is similar to the face mask on a football helmet.

GLOVES
You just gotta have.
ELBOW PADS
You just gotta have.
KNEE GUARDS
You just gotta have.
SHIN GUARDS
And you just gotta have.
MOUTH GUARD
Necessary for league play.
CUP
For the guys.
PADDED HOCKEY PANTS
Not crucial but butt slams are frequent and painful.
HOCKEY SHOULDER PADS
Hey, pads make better shock absorbers than body parts.

GOALIES HAVE EVEN MORE STUFF!
CAGE MASK
Gotta Have. Keeps the pucks out of your eyes. Make sure it's approved for puck play.
CHEST PROTECTOR
Gotta Have. Pucks will land here.
LEG PADS
Gotta have. Like mini-billboards.
GOALIE GLOVE
Gotta have. Like a gargantuan catcher's mitt.
GOALIE STICK
Gotta have. Has mega-size blade.

Chapter Eight

***Geared and Equipped for Street Hockey*--** *Helmet, elbow pads, gloves, and shin guards. The best stuff is light and fits so well you forget it's even there. His equipment provides protection as well as the confidence to play hard.*

Hockey Gear

Darth Vader-- Or, the goalie wears alotta stuff. And so would you if four players were trying to shoot a puck down your throat!

BLOCKER

A big, fat pad that attaches to the stick arm.

Used stuff is OK as long as it works.

Take your protection seriously. Street hockey is not a gentle sport and the surface is hard. Your salesperson will know about the name brands. Buy those. You'll play safer, tougher, and more confidently.

SKATES

You *can* play in your knock-around skates. You don't need to buy hockey skates, per se. However, hockey-specific skates are stiffer and more durable than recreational skates, and are the overwhelming choice for serious players. **As discussed in the first chapter, your skates do need to provide solid support and comfort.**

The kind of wheels you should have depends on the surface you end up playing on. **See *More About Wheels* in chapter one.**

THE STICK

Besides the skates, the stick is a hockey player's most valued tool. It always stays in your mitts. Always.

Sticks range in price from $10 to $200. There are conventional wood shafted sticks, as well as fiberglass reinforced wood, aluminum, graphite, and carbon fiber shafts that you can put replacement blades in. The Cadillac of the industry has an ABS plastic blade wrapped with fiberglass that boasts the longest, most even wear of them all.

Don't buy the sticks with the plastic blade glued/screwed on the end. They're cheap but the blade bends too much. And they're horribly unhip. When you play this game (or any other game for that matter) you

Hockey Gear

Hockey Skates--
The very best hockey skates are lace-up in order to provide the firmest foot and ankle support possible. They are built to take a higher degree of punishment and come with special wheels made to play this lightening fast game.

The Stick-- *Make sure your stick has an ABS plastic blade reinforced with fiberglass.*

Take the same care in purchasing a stick as you did with your skates. It will become like a body part during the game.

Chapter Eight

***Fitting the Stick*--**
The first thing you do with your fresh stick is to saw it to size. With the blade resting on the surface, the top of the handle should arrive somewhere between mid-chest and chin with skates on.

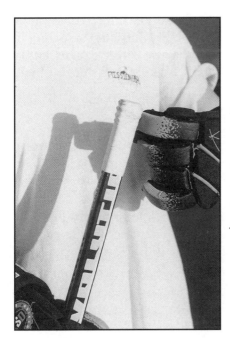

***Taping the Stick*--**
Taping the handle provides grip. Building up a knob with tape provides a stop for your hand and makes the stick easier to pick up from the pavement.

Hockey Gear

gotta roll into it with some bluster. You can't pretend to be THE GREAT ONE with a flyswatter.

FITTING THE STICK

The first thing you do with your brand new stick (again, old and beat-up is fine if it works) is saw it in half. Well, not quite in half. **Saw off the handle so that its butt end reaches somewhere between chest and chin when you stand the stick in front of you, with your skates on. If you're not wearing skates, measure to the tip of your nose.**

If the handle is longer than this the stick will have a tendency to buck the blade toe-up when you work the puck (dribble) along the surface. If the handle is too short the blade will buck heel-up. **The blade should always rest flush to the playing surface to maximize its striking area.**

You can tape the handle to improve your grip (it's something of a tradition in some circles). And you can tape a knob at its end to make a grip stop. Or you can buy a rubber knob that'll do the same thing. The knob is a good idea because it makes dropped sticks so much easier to retrieve from the playing surface. The knob gives the handle a bit of height, making it easier to pluck off the pavement.

BALL OR PUCK

Street hockey is played with a puck on smooth surfaces, or with a special ball on rough pavement. To keep the text simple the scoring object will be referred to as the puck only.

A roller hockey puck isn't like an ice hockey puck. It has runners, wheels, or bearings to make it slide on the pavement. The Jofa Speed Puck is the official puck of Roller Hockey International (RHI).

the game/9

SOME BASICS

Roller Hockey, of course, is very similar to ice hockey. Two teams glide about furiously and each tries to knock a puck into the other's net or goal. The nets are placed on either side of the playing surface. Each team has a net to defend and a net to shoot into. Players use a hockey stick to control the puck. The object is to score more goals (hitting the puck into the net) than the other team within a certain time frame.

There are three major points of difference outside of the wheels-on-pavement versus blades-on-ice:

1) **Roller hockey does not allow checking** or body blocking.

2) **Roller hockey does not have any line calls.** There are no offside and/or icing rules (players can be and/or shoot anywhere most anytime).

3) **Roller hockey requires five players per team** versus six for ice hockey.

The Game

These differences make roller hockey an extremely fast, wide-open game that emphasizes individual skating and stick handling expertise over size and strength. It's fun to watch and exhilarating to play.

Games usually consist of two action-packed 15 minute halves that largely consist of a blur of end-to-end rushes with alotta scoring. (The time per period can vary from age group to age group).

POSITIONS

Of the five players on each team, two or three are offensive players, two or three are defensive players, and one is the goaltender or goalie. The offensive positions spearhead the scoring drives and shoot the most at the other team's net. The defensive positions hang back a bit, help set up the offensive players, and are always prepared to guard their team's net. The goalie always parks himself in front of his team's net to block the opposing team's scoring attempts.

Since the game is rather wide-open, offensive and defensive responsibilities aren't set in stone. All players except the goalie can and should be able to score or defend at a moment's notice. There are strategies, especially at the higher skill levels in organized competition, but nothing as structured as football, basketball, or even ice hockey.

TEAMWORK

Despite the lack of scripted plays, however, it does require alotta team effort to be successful.

Each and every player must develop a vision of the field of play. That is, each player should know where everyone is all the time in order to move and control the puck or to properly defend against an onslaught. It isn't a free-for-all even though it certainly seems like it is sometimes.

Chapter Nine

Passing is a very big deal in winning hockey. Even the best skaters and puck handlers can't always break away to score on their own. They'll get crowded by the opposing team and lose the puck. It's more effective to keep the puck moving up the rink, from one open team mate to the next, until a scoring opportunity close to the net presents itself.

The defending team not only goes for the guy with the puck, but keeps an eye on all the members of the advancing team in order to prevent one of them from getting too open for a pass.

So the game is a blend of individual skills bound by team effort. It becomes more fun to play and watch as skating and stick handling improves among all individual team members, and reaches an entirely new level when players become increasingly aware of the presence and value of their team mates.

The Game

*Teamwork is essential in winning hockey. You gotta know where everybody is all the time. And players must **pass, pass, pass!***

hockey skating skills/10

Skating is the most basic of the two basic skills in this sport. Just to keep up, **players must eventually learn how to start and stop quickly, turn either way, and execute crossover turns either way. That's forwards and backwards.**

Yikes!

Yeah, that's a tall order when you're still wobbly just standing there, but as previously stated, you'll get better fast as you play. You can't help yourself!

REVIEW

Go back over the first part of this book for the basic skating skills. And keep three things in mind:

1) YOU CAN DO IT!

This is not pep talk (well, maybe a little). Before you can learn anything, you have to have the confidence that you indeed are capable of learning. *(What?)*

Learning how to travel on wheels is not easy for

alotta folks and some of the more advanced skills are a challenge for anybody. But it can be done. **You must convince yourself that you are able to learn.** It may take a heck of a lot of effort and time but it ain't like you're trying to fly off a bridge. Sure, right now it seems impossible to execute backwards crossovers, but it isn't. Lots of folks more clumsy than you picked it up. Just keep at it.

2) RHYTHM

Everything about skating is rhythmic. **Each skill has a groove that feels natural when you do it right.** It flows. And when you finally get it, bingo!, along comes confidence. Skating can become as natural and comfortable as a walk around the park.

3) SKATING ON ONE FOOT

Right from the start develop the skill and confidence to skate-your-weight on one foot. And I don't mean like a figure skater with one leg swung out back. When you stroke either forwards or backwards, during crossovers and/or transitions, one foot and then the other steers the ship. For that nano-second you're skating on one foot.

It's central to everything. Each foot should be able to control your skating destiny at a moments notice.

Here's some new stuff:

READY POSITION

When you're just standing there, before you commence to zooming around (like during a face-off or any break in the action), assume the *ready position*:

Skates are shoulder width apart, slightly splayed out, knees are bent, chest and head are up, and arms are loose in front of you.

POWER START

From the ready position, lean forward from the hips

Chapter Ten

Ready Position-- *Poised for action. Toes are pointed out a bit and the knees are turned in slightly in order insure a fast start. The stick is held loosely out in front with the blade flush to the playing surface.*

Hockey Skating Skills

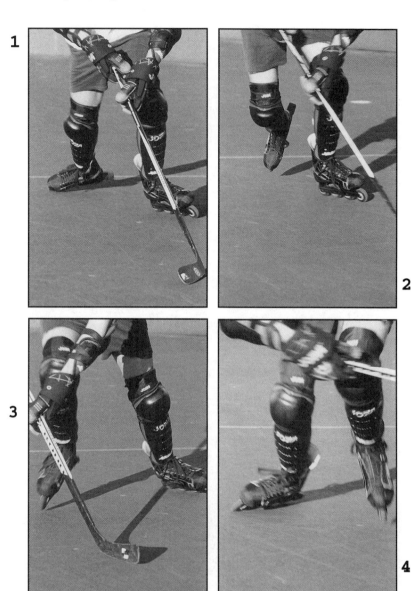

Power Start *(left to right)-- From a ready position, the entire row of wheels on each skate digs into the pavement at almost a right angle to the forward motion.*

Chapter Ten

(keep your head up), and start running from the splayed or **V** position your feet should already be in. **Push off from the center of each foot using the entire row of wheels.** You'll sorta clip-clop along at first until you get your speed up. Then smooth it out with a power stroke...

POWER STROKE

...is just a concentrated, pumped-up stroke. **During each stroke, push off on the entire row of wheels and bring the skate completely back below your hips.** To get more speed and power, bend your knees and straighten your leg after each stroke.

POWER TURN

Point your knees, inside foot, and inside shoulder in the direction you wish to turn. As you turn, bend your knees and roll your knees and ankles into the pavement. Meanwhile, move your lead (inside) skate ahead of the other.

This ain't easy. Practice this one with pads and pillows.

As mentioned in chapter one, rockering the wheels of your skates will make them even more turnable. Since only two of your wheels are meeting the surface at any one time, the radius of your turns decreases dramatically. Rockering does take some time getting used to, as it will make your skates seem real squirrely at first.

POWER CROSSOVERS

This is the crossover turn which was covered in the *Skating Part*. Only going faster. As you cross over, really push off those edges. **You'll actually build up speed during this turn so it's important to keep yourself over the wheels and commit.** (Whenever the *commit*

Hockey Skating Skills

Power Stroke *(left to right)-- Pushing hard through the entire row of wheels on each skate. Each stroke begins with the knee sharply bent underneath the hips and ends with a straight leg.*

Chapter Ten

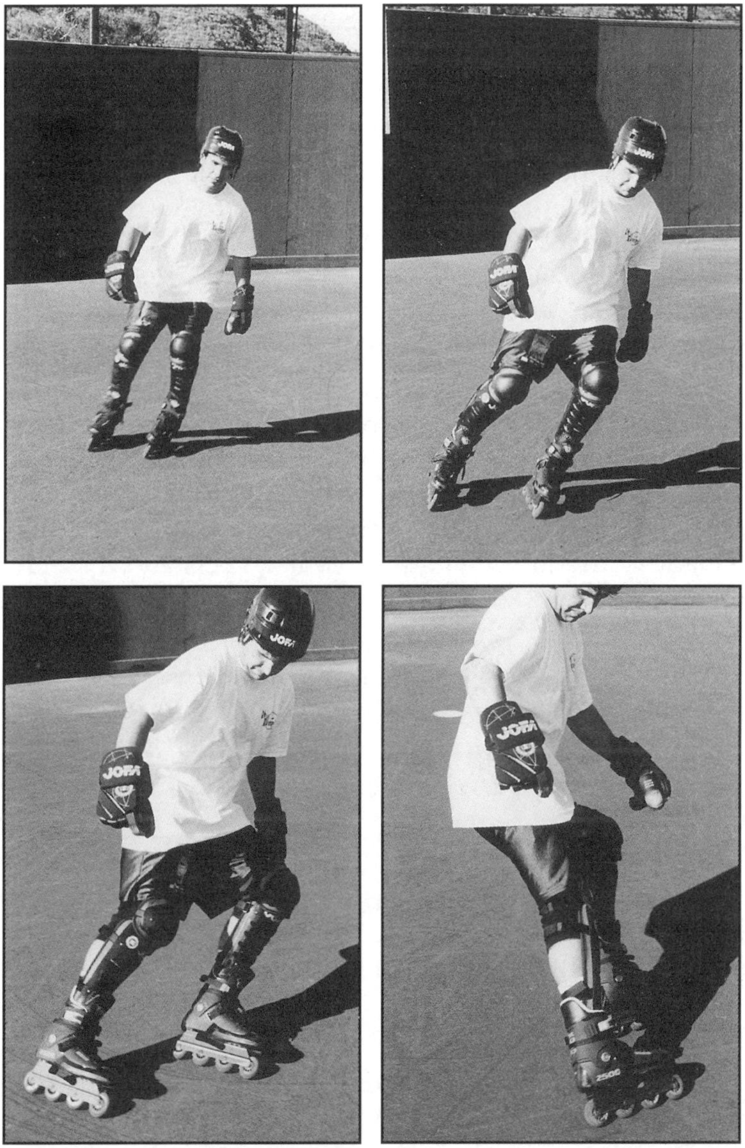

Power Turn *(left to right)-- Knees turn into the pavement and the legs scissor to accentuate the change in direction.*

87

word appears, that means ya gotta want it or else.

POWER STOPS

HOCKEY STOP

Go into a power turn, extend the outside skate out, lay that skate practically on its side, commit your weight to it, and slide to a halt on the inside edges of your wheels and the side of your skate. **Note the *commit* word here. Practice accordingly. A mis-cue with this maneuver can wreck an ankle.**

POWER SLIDE

Sorta like the hockey stop except the inside skate is turned around heel-first, in line with the gliding stop. That leg is bent at the knee while the braking leg and skate are extended as before. Again, **commit** your weight to the inside edges of your wheels and the side of your skate.

STOPPING BACKWARDS

SNOWPLOW

From a backwards glide, simply bring your heels together, splay your skates out, and lean forward. This one's a snap.

POWER SLIDE

Like its forward-looking brother, one skate is extended to brake (in a very committed fashion) while the other glides behind with bended knee.

PARTING SHOTS

Get into the habit of practicing with all your pads and eventually your hockey stick as well. After all, that's how you're gonna play. However, **learn how to execute these skating skills without a stick at first. There's a tendency to use the stick as a crutch when you first stumble around and that impedes true proficiency.**

Chapter Ten

Hockey Stop *(left to right)-- The moves are much the same as a power turn. Instead of completing the turn, extend the leg out and slide to a halt on the inside edge of your wheels and the side of the skate.*

Hockey Skating Skills

Power Slide *(left to right)-- Much like the hockey stop except for the positioning of the back skate. And like the hockey stop, a rather difficult maneuver to master.*

Chapter Ten

Speed will come over time. As will execution. What'll break you today will become a smooth move tomorrow. Don't give up.

And playing the game is the best way to get better by a long shot!

Backwards Snowplow--
Stopping yourself going backwards is as easy as bringing your heels together and leaning forward.

This is a heck of a way to end a chapter. Is this the best tush we could find?

Hockey Skating Skills

The other basic skill in hockey is stick handling. It's the only way a player can move the puck. And moving the puck is what this game is all about.

Like the skates are to the feet, the stick is to the arms. Both will become extensions of your mind and body. You simply won't have the time to think about 'em during a game.

THE GRIP

Put on your gloves. Grab hold of the stick with both hands. One hand holding the butt, the other about a foot and a half down on the shank. Rest the stick in your fingers and take a few forehand swings (forehand swings out in front of you, with the curve of the blade). Now reverse the position of your hands and take a few forehand swings the other way.

Which feels better?

OK. That's the way you'll hold the stick for all time.

On the Stick

Gripping the Stick *(left to right)-- The pix tell the story. This is how the stick is held 90% of the time. Only during the harder shots is the stick held tighter with hands farther apart.*

And you'll never, ever switch during a game. It's gotta be like it's glued there.

Back to the basic grip. The top hand fingers the butt of the stick firmly, the lower hand fingers the handle just a little more loosely. **Except when you're shooting at the goal, this is pretty much how you grip the stick. Firm on top, looser on the bottom, about a foot and one-half apart.**

This grip will enable you to send off a pass with a deft touch, and receive a pass with soft hands. With a tighter grip, the hands lose their sensitivity and send off harder, less accurate passes. A tighter grip also tends to bounce a pass off the blade instead of catching it.

When you shoot at the goal, especially with the more powerful shots, your grip will be firmer and your lower hand farther down the handle.

DRIBBLING

The first stick skill to learn is called dribbling. This is how you propel the puck up the rink. You don't just push, shove, or drag it around because it's too easy for the defense to steal. Dribbling is constantly moving the puck to-and-fro as you move it along.

You can do it in front of yourself or to either side. In all cases, as you do this to-and-fro thing, you angle the blade over the puck to better fend off a steal. Angling the blade in this manner allows you to maintain a down pressure on the stick that an opponent cannot easily disrupt.

Dribbling is a touch skill that involves rolling the wrists and shushing the puck ever-so-lightly back and forth with the tip of the blade. And that means touch as in not looking down at the puck when you're doing it.

You can't look for passing and/or scoring opportunities and elude the defense while you're staring at the

On the Stick

Dribbling *(left to right)-- This is how you move around with the puck. You don't just drag it or hit it along. You sorta feather it back and forth with the tip of your blade. And don't stare at the puck. Learn how to dribble with your head up.*

Chapter Eleven

bouncing puck at your feet. Dribbling must become second nature, as in basketball.

IT'S NOT A WEAPON!

Learn it now and forever. Keep your stick low. The stick is made to move a puck only. Any other use is probably a penalty and more important, a very real danger.

Whenever you handle the puck, the blade of your stick should angle or cup over it. This makes it harder for the defense to steal.

On the Stick

passing/12

Passing is the most effective way to move the puck. There are times when a player can make a run at the goal and shoot all on his own, but it just doesn't happen very often. It would be like a quarterback in football making a run for it from a straight snap from center without passing the ball, or handing it off, or waiting for his blocks to set up. Unless the defense makes some huge mistakes, he's gonna get creamed every time.

Same thing in hockey. One dribbling player making a break for the goal will get hopelessly swarmed by the defense and lose the puck for sure.

Passing not only moves the puck at great speeds, but breaks up defenses as well. An offense that passes alot and does it well can keep any defense guessing as to where the puck will be next. Sooner or later holes will appear in the defensive front that can be exploited.

Passing

And passing is a ton of fun! Finding that open team mate and feeding him that perfect pass is really a charge. Especially if it leads to an ideal scoring opportunity.

Passing is the heart of this game and every player needs to get good at it.

PASSING BASICS

Passing is a finesse skill. Except when you're clearing the puck from an area of the rink and you don't care where it goes, you're trying to move the puck to a given teammate who is probably on the move. Of course, you're in motion as well, so hitting him with a quick, accurate pass in stride is no simple matter. In fact, it's a higher art form.

In general, maintain a soft lower hand and a firm upper when passing or receiving. When you make your pass, make sure you lead your receiver and aim for his/her stick. **Don't whack the puck.** In most cases, you begin the pass with the blade of your stick cradling the puck. **The hitting motion is more of a sweep with varying degrees of power, blade angle, and follow-through.** Look where you're passing before you pass and point to your target with the blade of your stick as you follow-through.

SHOVEL PASS

Or cut pass. Use this pass when your receiver is close by and relatively clear. It's something of a touch pass and does not require much power. It's a highly accurate way to move the puck and should be a mainstay in your arsenal of skills.

Cradle the puck towards the heel of your blade and angle the blade towards the puck. Then simply push the puck towards the stick of your receiver with little or no follow-through. That is, keep your blade low to the surface after you push the puck.

Chapter Twelve

Passing Grip-- *The stick is held with a firm upper hand and a looser lower hand.*

The relaxed grip provides the passer with a softer touch and the receiver with softer hands.

Leading a receiver-- *Hitting a team mate with a pass while you're both on the move is a superior skill.*

As in football, the passer must lead his receiver. Aim for the blade, not the body.

Passing

Sweeping it is more accurate than belting it-- *Passing does not entail striking the puck. Passing is a sweeping motion that begins with the blade of the stick cradling the puck..*

Open Blade-- *The blade is angled away from the puck. This will lift the puck into the air when swept or struck.*

Closed Blade-- *The blade is angled toward the puck. This will keep the puck on the surface.*

This pass will stay on the surface and go exactly in the direction it was shoved.

FLIP PASS

As the name implies, this pass leaves the surface but it does not flip, per se, if it's a puck. It should sail in a flat spin. Use this pass when you need to clear skates and sticks in the immediate vicinity in order to hit your receiver. You will use a bit more power in your initial sweep of the puck, but if executed properly, it should be a very accurate pass.

Cup the puck at the middle of your blade and angle the blade away from the puck. This is called an open blade. **Give the puck a firm sweep and a flick of the wrists to give it some air.** Ideally you want the puck to slide off the blade from its middle to the toe. This and the wrist flick gives the puck its spin and is crucial to an accurate pass if you're playing with a puck.

Your follow-through should not be higher than a foot or so above the surface. Anything higher than that will ruin the chances of an accurate, spinning puck. A high follow-through will cause the puck to spin end-over-end and chances are it will land on its end and bounce every-which-way. The puck or ball should travel a foot or so above the surface for about ten feet exactly in the direction in which it was hit.

LIFT PASS

Use this pass to simply clear the puck from a given area. It's usually used when the puck is dangerously close to the net you're defending and there's no other way to salvage the situation. Accuracy is very marginal.

With an open blade, sweep the puck from the toe of your blade with a powerful stoke. Use a high follow-through and watch this one fly. The higher the follow through, the higher the puck will sail. This pass will

Passing

Shovel Pass-- This is just a push pass. The puck is gently swept along with a closed blade.

The follow-through is low in order to keep the puck on the surface.

Chapter Twelve

Flip Pass *(clockwise)-- Also known as the saucer pass because of its flat spin and trajectory. The puck is firmly swept with an open blade. The follow-through is about a foot off the surface.*

Note how Randy points towards his target.

Passing

Lift Pass *(clockwise)-- This is a clearing pass used when the puck needs to travel high and far. Accuracy is minimal. The puck is swept forcefully with an open blade. The high follow-through gives it height.*

enable you to pass over the heads of players.

DROP PASS

This is an extremely effective pass and simple to do. As you dribble up the rink with a team mate close behind, simply stop dribbling and leave the puck behind for him to pick up. Since the defense will be anticipating your forward motion with the puck, oft times they will be caught off guard with this ploy.

BOARD PASS

If you're playing in a rink with boards circling the area, you can bounce a pass off the boards, through or around a defender, to another team mate, or yourself. It's kinda like playing pool.

BACKHAND PASSES

All of these passes can be executed from the back of the blade or your backhand. Using the back of the blade is more difficult because the puck isn't cupped inside the curve of the blade. You have to deal with a striking surface that's curved out and considerably more unwieldy to use. It does take some time getting used to.

But you'll find yourself getting used to it real fast because half the time that's where the puck will be. **You simply cannot position yourself for forehand passing/receiving/shooting every single time.** Remember, you don't switch hands on your stick (you'd be too vulnerable while you switched). So unless they let you call time out every time you find the puck on your backhand, you better learn how to deal with a convex blade!

Basically your backhands are the same as your forehand passes except you're pulling with your lower hand instead of pushing.

Passing

1

2

3

***Backhand Pass*--** *Using the back or convex side of the blade, the puck is swept with a pulling motion. More or less the same technique is used to execute the backhand shot.*

RECEIVING

Think soft hands when receiving a pass. Hold the stick loosely with your bottom hand with the blade flush against the surface. As the puck arrives, pull back a bit and catch it, absorbing the shock in your hands and arms.

The puck will not stick to a rigid blade. If the stick is tightly held, and/or not brought back with the reception, the puck will bounce off. The more rigid the receiving surface, the greater the bounce.

Passing

shooting/13

After all, goals win games. Getting the puck into the net is how you score the goals. How you put it there is all about shooting.

SHOOTING BASICS

Shooting usually requires a firmer grip with the lower hand. Except for the slide shot, you're gonna need a little muscle. **For power, move your lower hand towards the middle of the handle.**

Before you shoot, look at your goal, then look at the puck, and look up again as you shoot and follow-through.

As in the passes, an open blade will force high shots, while an angled-in blade will keep shots low or on the surface.

Hit the puck with the middle of the blade and slide it off the toe for spin and accuracy. Point towards the goal with the blade of your stick during the follow-through.

There are four basic shots. They are progressively more difficult to master and less accurate the harder you hit the puck.

Shooting

***Shooting Grip*--** *For the harder hit shots, the stick is held with a firmer grip. The lower hand grips the handle towards the middle of the stick.*

Whether passing or shooting, the blade of your stick should point towards your target during the follow-through. The higher the follow-through, the greater the lift.

Chapter Thirteen

SLIDESHOT

This shot is used when a deft touch is in order. Like the shovel pass, you just sorta push the puck into the net.

WRISTSHOT

This shot is most effective within 25 feet of the net. **It's probably the most effective shot you'll have in your quiver of skills.**

With the puck somewhat behind you, sweep the puck along and transfer your weight from back to front skate. Keep the blade in contact with the puck. **As you send the shot off, snap your wrists sharply. Keep your follow-through low to keep the puck on the surface. Higher to give it some air.**

SNAPSHOT

This shot leaves the surface in a flat spin. **Raise the stick about two feet or so above the surface behind the puck and snap down.** Again transferring your weight from rear to front. Shoot through the puck and keep your follow-through low. **Allow the puck to slide off the toe of the blade. This is what gives it its spin and accuracy.** The puck should travel about two to three inches off the surface.

SLAPSHOT

The most dramatic and powerful shot. Also the least accurate and most difficult to master.

With the puck just ahead of the front skate, raise the stick high in the wind-up, snap down, and shoot through the puck. Transfer your weight sharply from back to front skate and make a full follow-through.

Shooting and keeping your balance while you're doing it is no small deal. Especially with the higher octane shots. Plant yourself with skates slightly wider than shoulder width, with knees bent.

Shooting

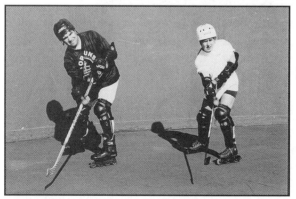

***Slideshot*--** *This is a touch shot that is so similar to the shovel pass in technique that they're more or less the same. Although lacking in dramatics, this is a very accurate shot. It is especially useful near the net.*

Chapter Thirteen

1

2

3

***Wristshot** (left to right)-- Again, no wind-up. A very firm sweep and a snap of the wrists propels this shot. The follow-through shown here is low in order to keep the puck on the surface. Probably the most reliable and useful shot of them all.*

Shooting

1

2

3

Snapshot *(left to right)-- This shot has a wind-up. Raise the stick about two feet and snap through the puck. Keep the follow-through around a foot or so above the surface. Like the flip or saucer pass, you want the puck to travel in a flat spin.*

Chapter Thirteen

Slapshot *(left to right)-- Big wind-up and big follow-through. Hands are definitely farther apart on this booming shot. As dramatic as this is, it's the least accurate of all the shots.*

Shooting

BACKHAND SHOTS

It ain't any easier shooting this way than it is to pass or receive. But it's good to know for the same reason: *you can't dictate where the puck is gonna land.* **If you find yourself with nothing but a backhand shot available, you gotta know how to make it!**

Again, it's a pulling motion that directs the stick.

defensive stick skills/14

When the other side has the puck, you try to get it back!

And **to play defense well, you gotta know how to skate backwards. That's the only way you can face a puck handler, block his way, and make an attempt to steal the puck.**

Otherwise you're skating alongside the opposing player with the puck, and from there you can't really do any of these things very well at all. The better you can skate backwards, the better you can play defense.

There are three basic ways to steal a puck with your stick:

STICK LIFT

Simply slip your stick underneath the puck handler's stick and lift up. This frees the puck for you or a team mate.

Defensive Stick Skills

1

2

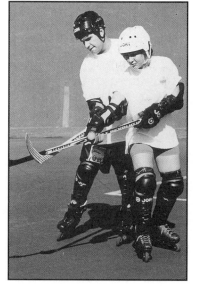

3

Stick Lift *(Clockwise)-- One of the most simple and effective of the stealing techniques. Once you have gained control of the offensive player's stick in this manner, the puck is yours!*

Chapter Fourteen

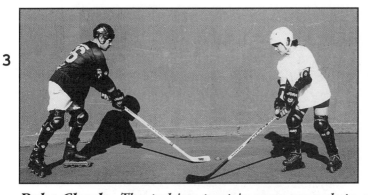

***Poke Check*--** *The poking part is easy enough to execute. It's the skating that's a challenge. In order to maintain the best position on a charging offensive player, the defenseman must be able to skate backwards well.*

Defensive Stick Skills

1

2

3

***Sweep Check*--** *Again the best position to execute this check is in front of the offensive player. And the only way to be there is by skating backwards effectively.*

POKE CHECK

Holding the butt of the handle for maximum extension, reach into the dribbling area of the puck handler and poke the puck free.

SWEEP CHECK

Lay your stick flush to the surface and sweep through the puck handler's dribbling area in order to free the puck.

Defensive Stick Skills

the goalie/15

My goodness! We've come this far and haven't once mentioned the over-dressed player standing in front of the net.

The goalie doesn't get to tear around the rink and score goals. **He pretty much has to stay in the one spot and block shots. But what moves a goalie *does* make are extremely crucial.**

Although the goalie doesn't have a particularly glamorous job, he will receive no lack of attention during the course of a game, and always plays an integral role in its outcome. In fact, the goalie often winds up the hero if he courageously defends the net from those thundering breakouts time after time. But of course it only takes one sneaky goal to lose a game and guess who's easiest to blame for that?

What price glory? Ask a goalie. They pay for it all the time.

The Goalie

In general, a goalie:

1) Inhibits the opposing shooter by **blocking his vision of the net.**

2) **Blocks the shot** in a variety of ways we'll get into soon.

3) **Captures or re-directs the puck to a team mate** in order to repossess the puck for his team.

STAMINA

The goalie wears a ton of stuff and wields some pretty cumbersome tools-of-the-trade. Because he must remain in the *ready position* (bent at the knees, slightly crouched, stick and glove poised, with head and shoulders up, and facing the action at all times) it takes mucho stamina to play at this position.

GUTS

Not a position for the faint-hearted. It does take a certain something to relish the charge of hurtling bodies and flying pucks. But with the proper protection, the goalie is no more at risk than any of the other players.

WHO IS THAT?

The preferred hand wears the goalie glove that is used to catch and pluck up the puck. The other hand holds the stick and on that arm he wears a blocker. Strapped to the legs are the leg pads, and underneath the jersey are the chest protector and shoulder pads. Over the head goes the helmet and cage, and there you have it. **The (wo)man from Mars.**

THE READY POSITION

The glove is held out in a 3 o'clock position that can adjust to high or low shots quickly. The stick is held at the juncture between blade and handle, with blade turned sideways/in, and flush to the surface. The blade is

Chapter Fifteen

Ready Position (in and out of position)-- *Although all three pix show the goalie poised in the proper ready position or stance, in the bottom two he is not covering this shooter's angle very well. There's much too much open net. This is a common error made by green goalies. The goalie must be a student of angles in order to protect his net.*

The Goalie

Cutting the Angle *(from left to right)-- From a shooter's perspective. As the goalie positions himself farther from the net, there's less and less net to see and shoot at. Obviously the goalie must be aware of just how far he can roam and still recover.*

positioned a few inches in front of the skates in order to give it room to catch and absorb the incoming puck.

Everything (glove, blocker, stick, and leg pads) faces out towards the action, all the time. And remember the killer stance: *skates shoulder width, knees bent, slight crouch, head and shoulders up.*

STAND PUT

As a rule, goalies always stay up on their skates unless there's no other way to block a shot. **The game is too quick and the puck moves too fast to be scrambling up and down on skates.**

PLAYING LARGE

Before a goalie actually blocks a shot, he blocks the view of an incoming shooter by what is called *cutting the angle.* The goalie places himself between the shooter and the net in such a way that most of the net is hidden from view. Oft times that means the goalie advances towards the shooter to make himself bigger to the shooter.

A goalie must know just how far he can advance and still retreat to the mouth of the net without serious consequence.

BASIC BLOCKS

When the shot is made there are eight basic ways to make the block or save:

GLOVE SAVE

The surest way to make a save is catching it in your glove. It's usually a goalie's best hand, hence the easiest to control. Since the puck is caught, not merely blocked, the goalie has immediate possession for his/her team and can quickly pass off to a team mate.

STICK SAVE

Using the flat of the huge blade on the goalie stick, a

The Goalie

Glove Save

Stick Save

Blocker Save

Leg Pad Save

Saves are Us-- This page and the next two demonstrate how it's done.

Chapter Fifteen

Kick Save

Toe Save

Body Save

The Goalie

Skate Save

So you wanna be a goalie. Well, try it on for size! Just make sure you bring a large enough moving van.

goalie either stops the incoming ball/puck or rebounds it to a team mate or to a clear area away from the net. You stop the puck by angling the blade towards the surface so that it falls in front of you for a quick scoop. To rebound the puck, hold the stick firmly and angle it toward the direction you want it to go.

BLOCKER SAVE

Using the face of the blocker, either stop or rebound the puck in the same manner as the stick save.

LEG PAD SAVE

Since the leg pads are the largest part of a goalie's apparel, they block the most shots. Because of their awkward size and weight they aren't utilized so much as a tool as are the glove, blocker, or stick. **Basically you're just trying to get them in front of an incoming shot by sliding to and fro. Always keep the pads facing out, and when you slide, move laterally across the goal.**

KICK SAVE

This is something of a desperation block because you end up on your knees and there you're vulnerable to attack. If a puck is sailing in at 8-18 inches off the surface towards a far side of the goal and there's nothing else you can do, throw a leg pad out to meet it. **It's crucial that you time the thrust with the arrival of the puck since there's no time to adjust.**

TOE SAVE

Again, you're thrusting a leg pad out there to stop a puck but this time you're on your knees and your skate stays on the ground. This is what you do, for example, after you've stopped one shot with a kick save but it has rebounded back to an offensive shooter and the son-of-a-gun is belting another one back at you. You're on your knees from the effort and all you can do is thrust out another leg.

The Goalie

The goalie must take care to block the open area between the splayed legs with stick and glove.

SKATE SAVE

This save is usually used to block very low or surface shots on the stick or weak side of the goalie where the glove and/or leg pads won't reach.

From a kneeling position, turn your skate sideways and block the shot with the row of wheels. **Note that this save leaves a very large gap in between the legs that is very difficult to protect.**

BODY SAVE

And when nothing else will work, just toss yourself in the path of the puck. **Another desperation save.**

LOOK 'EM IN THE EYE

A goalie never anticipates a shooter's move. He waits for the shooter to commit and then commits to the puck.

KEEP YOUR AREA TIDY

When pucks are sailing around your area unattended and you can get to them without jeopardizing your position, haul them in and pass them off to a team mate.

playing the game/16

The game flows from one end of the rink to the other. One team has the puck and takes it towards the other team's goal in order to shoot it in and score a goal. The team without the puck tries to block this advance and tries to steal the puck back. The team with the puck either scores or loses the puck and the situation is reversed. The action then flows toward the other end of the rink.

As mentioned earlier, **the best way to move the puck is usually by making sharp and accurate passes to team mates who are breaking clear, while moving ever closer to the other team's goal.**

There are times when a player can dribble all the way up a rink by himself and make a scoring attempt without assistance, but that's the exception rather than the rule. As it is in basketball.

The best offenses are team efforts. Players are

aware of the movements of each of their team mates and pass the puck along with just one purpose: to create scoring opportunities.** The best defenses are adept at blocking and stealing the puck with the skills described in the *Defensive Stick Skills* chapter. More than that, however, **the best defenses always have an eye on each offensive player to prevent breakaways.** The defense never wants to allow an offensive player to break free for a pass.

So in order to play the best offense or defense, players must have an awareness of the entire field of play. Not only do they have to know what their own team is doing, but they must know what the other team is up to as well.

Since the puck can change sides in the blink of an eye, this vision of the field of play is crucial to winning hockey. Although so much of this game depends on individual skills and effort, in the end it's the interaction of players that makes the whole thing flow. Or break apart for the lack of it.

To help organize the offensive and defensive efforts on each team there are three positions of basic responsibility: the goalie, the two forwards, and the two defensemen. The goalie we already talked about.

FORWARDS

The basic responsibility of the forward position is to receive passes and score goals. So they must be skilled at this. They must also be terrific skaters in order to get into scoring position in the first place. Forwards spearhead any attack towards the goal.

It is also a forward's role to face-off with the other team's forward to start play. In a face-off, the referee drops the puck in between the two players who try to backhand the puck to a team mate.

Chapter Sixteen

DEFENSEMEN

Defensemen feed passes to the forwards and keep an eye on the offensive movements of the other team. They're the best defensive stickmen on a given team, and the best backward skaters. Defensemen usually hang back a bit when their team is on the offensive in order to prevent breakaways by the other team.

Although their primary role is to defend and to support the scoring efforts of the forwards, defensemen should develop a strong slapshot in the event a scoring opportunity should present itself from their somewhat distant vantage.

Now these job descriptions are nice and neat, but the game is not. It's all over the place! In a split second the puck can change hands 2-3 times. **The pace of the game demands that each player be able to assume both offensive and defensive duties as the action dictates.**

And that's OK. It's just one more thing about this game that makes it so exciting and FUN!

BASIC STRATEGIES

In organized play there are two basic offensive plans:

THE BOX/DIAMOND

In the box, the two forwards and the two defensemen form a square or box and head up the rink towards the other team's goal. The forwards lead the way, the defensemen hang back. They pass along the way. When they arrive at the other end, they take turns cutting in at the net, trying to break free for a pass with which to shoot and score. Teams sometimes shift to a diamond at some point to further confuse the defense.

This is a tried and true, conservative scheme. Passes are short and safe, and it's easy to snap back quickly into a defensive mode if need be.

Playing the Game

THE BREAKOUT

From his own team's end of the rink, a defensemen either shoots a long pass to one of his team mates, who have scattered down the rink, or he dribbles it up-rink himself until someone gets open.

This is a much more wide open strategy that can break up a defense and score alotta points, and/or get a team in trouble because players have gotten themselves too far from defensive positions.

It's especially important that players in this strategy be aware of not only the whereabouts of team mates, but also of the whereabouts of opposing players who may be planning their own breakout.

AND THE MOST IMPORTANT THING

Have *Fun!*

Glossary

Backhand pass- Pass using the back or covex side of the blade on a hockey stick.

Backhand shot- Shot using the back or convex side of the blade on a hockey stick.

Bearings- The ring of ball bearings installed in each skate wheel. Either oil or grease packed. Quality rated as ABEC-1, -3, -5, or no rating.

Blade- On a hockey stick, the curved portion that strikes or sweeps the puck.

Block- The act of preventing a puck from entering a net by a goalie. A save.

Blocker- The large pad that fits on the arm of a goalie's stick hand.

Blocker save- Type of blocked shot by a goalie using the blocker.

Board pass- Pass that is intentionally bounced off the boards surrounding a rink.

Body save- Type of blocked shot by a goalie using his body.

Box/diamond strategy- An offensive scheme where the players form a box or diamond as they attack the opposing team's net.

Breakaway- When a player/players are able to break free with the puck and attack the opposition's net unguarded.

Breakout strategy- An offensive scheme where players aggressively skate at random trying to break free in order to receive long passes and score.

C Cutting- Skating backwards by pushing out, around and in on each skate in an alternating fashion.

Checking- Body blocking. Not allowed in roller hockey.

Core of wheel- The hub that surrounds the bearings.

Either open with spokes or holes, or closed and solid.

Crossovers- Turning technique where one skate advances and crosses over the other. Either forward or backward.

Cutting the angle- The positioning a goalie takes between a shooter and his net where the goalie's body blocks the shooter's view of the net.

Defensemen- One of the three positions on a roller hockey team. They generally pass to the forwards and stay back to defend their end of the rink.

Diameter of wheel- The size of a skate wheel. The larger the faster.

Dribbling- Advancing the puck by feathering it on either side of the blade of a hockey stick.

Drop pass- Pass where the puck is simply left behind in order that a team mate following might pick it up.

Durometer of wheel- The hardness of a skate wheel. Harder wheels are faster but provide less grip.

Face-off- Start of play where referee drops puck between opposing forwards.

Flip pass- Pass that is swept into a flat spin above the surface.

Forward- One of three positions on a roller hockey team. They generally take passes from the defensemen and try to score.

Glove save- When a goalie catches the puck with his glove to prevent a goal.

Goalie- One of three positions on a roller hockey team. The player who guards the net.

Hockey stop- Stopping technique where one skate is thrust out and slides on the inside edges of the wheels and the side of the skate.

Hockey vision- A player's ability to sense the whereabouts and intentions of all the players in the rink.

Glossary

***Hour glass*-** Skating backwards by pushing out, then in on both skates at the same time.

***Icing*-** In ice hockey, shooting the puck from one end of the playing area across the red, blue, and goal lines into the offensive zone. There is no such rule in roller hockey.

***Kick save*-** Type of blocked shot by a goalie using a thrusting leg.

***Kidstuff syndrome*-** A mental state that affects most in-line skaters. Characterized by a total lack of interest in the adult world view and an all-encompassing desire to have fun.

***Leg pad save*-** Type of blocked shot by a goalie using a leg pad.

***Lift pass*-** Pass that is swept high and far to clear an area.

***Offside rule*-** In ice hockey, when an offensive player precedes the puck across the blue line into the offensive zone. There is no such rule in roller hockey.

***Ol'in and out*-** Slowing technique where skates are spread apart and brought together again.

***Poke check*-** Stealing a puck by poking it away with a hockey stick.

***Power crossover*-** Just a pumped-up crossover.

***Power slide*-** Stopping technique using a thrusting sliding skate, as in the hockey stop, and turning the rear skate heel first.

***Power start*-** From a standstill, pushing hard off each row of wheels as they are positioned at almost right angles to the forward motion.

***Power stroke*-** Just a pumped up stroke. Super bent knees to straight legs on strokes.

***Power turn*-** A hard, tight turn made by leaning into the turn and separating the skates.

***Profile of wheel*-** The thickness of the wheel. The

thinner the faster. Thicker wheels are more stable.

***Puck*-** The flat, round scoring object. A ball can also be used in roller hockey.

***Ready position*-** Skates shoulder width, knees in and bent, slight crouch, arms and stick out front and loose.

Ready position (goalie)- Like the other ready position (above) with glove at 3 o'clock and all gear up and facing the action.

***Rockering of wheels*-** Dropping middle wheels on skates so wheels form an arch. Increases maneuverability.

***Rotating of wheels*-** Switching wheels around in order that they wear more evenly.

***Save*-** The act of preventing a goal by a goalie. A blocked shot.

***Shovel pass*-** A simple push pass.

***Slapshot*-** The most powerful shot in hockey. High wind-up and high follow-through.

***Slideshot*-** Or shovel shot. Simple touch shot.

***Snapshot*-** Shot with low wind-up and low follow-through.

***Snowplow*-** Stopping technique where skates are brought together toe-first and pressure is applied to the inside edges. In a backwards snowplow the heels of the skates are brought together.

***Stick*-** The hockey stick.

***Stick lift*-** Stealing technique where the stick of the puck handler is lifted by the stick of the defensemen.

***Stick save*-** Type of blocked shot by goalie using his stick.

***Stridenglide*-** A skater's stroke. Stride and glide.

***Stroke*-** The rhythmic striding and gliding of a skater.

***Sweep check*-** Stealing technique where puck is swept away from the blade of the puck handler with stick of the defensemen.

Glossary

T-stop- Stopping technique where skater places one skate behind another at a right angle and applies downward pressure.

Toe save- Type of blocked shot by a goalie using the outstretched toe of his skate.

Toe-stop- Like the T-stop except only using the front wheel of the dragging skate.

Transitions- Going forwards to backwards and/or backwards to forwards on skates.

Wristshot- Sweeping shot where wrists are snapped and follow-through is kept low to medium-high.

Resources

In-Line Skating Shops and Roller Hockey Shops
Look under skates/in-line in the yellow pages. These stores may or not be strictly in-line. They probably cater to other action/outdoor sport interests. But chances are a huge part of their business these days is in-line and roller hockey stuff. So they might be a great source for local information about:
> In-line skating/hockey areas and rinks
> In-line skating/hockey camps
> In- line skating/hockey lessons
> In-line skating/hockey contests and games
> In-line skating/hockey organizations

These stores should also provide:
> In-line skating/hockey gear
> In-line skaters/hockey players to talk to
> In-line skating/hockey literature and videos

In-Line Skating and Roller Hockey Magazines

Hockey Player Magazine
PO Box 7494
Northridge, CA 91327
1-800-807-2231

Hockey Talk Magazine
40575 California Oaks Road
#D2255
Murrieta, CA 92562
909-677-0464

InLine Magazine
2025 Pearl Street
Boulder, CO 80302
303-440-5111 Fax 303-440-3313

Roller Hockey Magazine
12327 Santa Monica Blvd. #202
Los Angeles. CA 90025
310-442-6660 Fax 310-442-6663

USA Hockey InLine Magazine
4965 North 30th Street
Colorado Springs, CA 80919
719-599-5500

Television
Check your listings. The professional roller hockey games of Roller Hockey International (RHI) are broadcast locally.

Videos
You can find them in the same stores that rent/sell skates or, of course, your neighborhood Blockbuster Video Monopoly.

<u>In-Line:</u>
Cyberskate–Action. Groove Productions.
Dare To Air– Action with Chris Edwards. Groove Productions.
Desmond's In-Line Skate Video– Action/instruction. Acculaw.
Get Started with Blading– Instruction with Joel Rappelfeld. Video Action Sports.
In-line In-shape– Instructional. Supreme Video Works.
Mad Beef: An In-Line Felony–Action. Video Action Sports.
Ride with The Best: The Athens to Atlanta Video. Footage from event. Hyperblue Productions.
SkateFit– Instruction/workout with Carolyn Bradley. ABA.

The Hoax: An In-Line Crime– Action. Video Action Sports.
Vertical Axis– Action/instruction. Kryptonics.
VideoGroove- Action. Groove Productions.
1994 The Flip Side– Action. Mar Productions.

<u>Roller Hockey:</u>
Roller Hockey: The Pro Approach– Instruction with Stephan Desjardins. Driscoll Communication.
Winning In-Line Hockey– Instruction with Herb Brooks. In-line Partners.

Organizations

American Youth Sports Foundation
PO Box 131
Solana Beach, CA 92075
619-632-0275

Berlin Hockey World, Inc.
109 East Chestnut Avenue
Berlin, NJ 08009
609-768-9015 FAX 609-768-9016

International In-Line Skating Association (IISA)
PO Box 15482
Atlanta, GA 30333
404-728-9707 Fax 404-728-9866

National In-Line Hockey Association (NIHA)
999 Brickell Avenue
9th Floor
Miami, FL 33131
800-358-6442 Fax 305-358-0046

USA Hockey In-Line
4965 North 30th Street
Colorado Springs, CO 80919
800-566-3288

United States Amateur Confederation of Roller Skating (USAC/RS)
4730 South Street
PO Box 6579
Lincoln, NB 68506
402-483-7551

Books
Blazing Bladers
By Bill Gutman
Tom Doherty Associates (1992)

Wheel Excitement
by Neil Feineman
Hearst Books (1991)

Movies
In *Airborne*, starring Shane McDermott, watch a transplanted California surfer dude become a skater dude and win the day and the girl. Hot skating by Team Rollerblade. Warner Brothers, 1993.

Bibliography

Brooks, Herb. *Winning In-Line Hockey (Video)*. Minneapolis, Minnesota: Greer and Associates/In-Line Hockey Partners.

Feineman, Neil. *Wheel Excitement*. New York, New York: Hearst Books, 1991.

Gutman, Bill. *Blazing Bladers*. New York, New York: Tom Doherty Associates, Inc.,1992.

InLine: The Skate Magazine. Boulder, Colorado: InLine Inc.

Zulewski, Richard. *The Parent's Guide to Coaching Hockey.* Cincinnati, Ohio: Betterway Books, 1993.

Index

Air bags 45
Backhand pass 107-108
Backhand shot 118
Backwards, skating 51-55
   C cutting 51, 53-54
   hour glass 51-52
Ball 76
Bearings 19-21
Blade:
   open 102
   closed 102
Blocks 129-132
Blocker 73
Blocker save 130, 133
Board pass 107
Body save 131, 134
Box/diamond strategy 137
Breakaway 138
Breakout strategy 138
Bunkum University 11
C Cutting 51, 53-54
Checking 77
Core of wheel 20
Crossovers:
   forward 47, 49-50
   backward 54-55
   power 85, 88
Cutting the angle 128-129
Defensemen 137
Defensive stick skills 119-123
Diameter of wheel 19
Dr. Timothy Schmitt 11

Dribbling 95-97
Drop pass 107
Durometer of wheel 20
Elbow pads 21
Face-off 82, 136
Falling 41-45
Fitness 11
Fleming, Peggy 63
Flip pass 103, 105
Follow-through 112
Forward 136
Fun 65-66
Gear:
   hockey 69-76
   skating 15-22
Glove save 129-130
Goalie 70, 72-73, 125-134
Heel Brake 38-40
Helmet:
   hockey 69-71
   skating 21
Hockey stop 88-89
Hockey vision 78-80, 136
Hour glass 51-52
Ice hockey 77
Icing 77
International In-Line Skate Association 23
Instruction 64
Kick save 131, 133
Kidstuff Syndrome 10-11
Knee pads 21
Koufax, Sandy 63

Index

Leading a receiver 100-101
Leg pad save 130, 133
Lift pass 103, 106-107
Michelin Man 45
Offside rule 77
Ol' in and out 34-35
Passing 78-80, 99-109
   grip for 100-101
Poke check 121, 123
Positions, hockey 78
Power crossover 85, 88
Power slide 88, 90
Power start 82, 84-85
Power stroke 85-86
Power stops 88-91
Power turn 85, 87
Profile of wheel 19
Protection:
   hockey 69-73
   skating 21
Puck 76
Ready position:
   goalie 126-127, 129
   hockey 82-83
Receiving a pass 109
Rockering of wheels 20, 22
Roller hockey 61-138
   game of 77-80, 135, 138
Rotating of wheels 21-22
Rules of the Road, skating 23
Safety 23-26
San Diego Roller Hockey Conference 66

Saves 129-132
Sex 64-65
Shooting 111-118
  grip for 111-112
Shovel pass 100, 103
Skate save 132, 134
Skates:
  buying 16-19
  fit 15-16
  hockey 73-74
  maintenance 21
  renting 15
Skating:
  in-line 7-59
  skills, hockey 81-91
Slapshot 113, 117
Slideshot 113-114
Slowing techniques 34-38
Snapshot 113, 116
Snowplow 34, 36, 88, 91
Stance, skating 27-29
Start-Up Books 13, 14
Stick, hockey:
  grip on 93-95
  handling 93-97
  hockey 73-76
  fitting 75-76
  taping 75-76
Stick lift 119-120
Stick save 129-130
Stopping:
  backward 88, 91

   hockey stop 88-89
   in-line skating 33-40
   power slide 88, 90
   power stops 88-91
Strategies 137-138
Stridenglide 29
Stroke:
   skating 30-32
   power 85-86
Sweep check 122-123
T-stop 39-40
Teamwork 79-80, 135-136
Ten commandments for parents 66
Toe save 131, 133-134
Toe-stop 39-40
Transitions 57-59
   forward to backward 58
   backward to forward 59
Turning:
   skating 47-50
   power 85, 87
Turn stop 37-38
Unitas, Johnny 63
University of Massachusetts 11
Vader, Darth 72
Wheels 19-21
   core of 20
   diameter of 19
   durometer of 20
   profile of 19
Wristguards 21
Wristshot 113, 115

Start-Up Sports

The *Start-Up Sports Series* was born of a Great Awakening. I woke up one morning and realized that I didn't like doin' what I was doin' anymore.

So I wrote a how-to book about surfing: *Surfer's Start-Up*.

They say if you're gonna write, you gotta write what you know about. And it helps if you have a passion for it. I surf everyday and love it, so that part was easy. Actually the whole writing, photo, editing, printing, distribution, promotion, and selling thing came together beautifully thanks to friends, family, and the stars.

So heck. I just kept at it. *Snowboarder's Start-Up, Sailor's Start-Up, In-Line Skater's Start-Up.* The books became my own personal **start-up** for changing my life. And making it meaningful and fun again.

Fun.

That's what these activities are and should be. That's what they're there for. And that's why they are so good for you, kids!

Here's my case. We all have to worry about *stuff*. Homework, mowing the lawn, jobs, MONEY, sleeping at night, retirement, sex, balding, dates, marriage, oil changes, etc. And all this *stuff* can get overwhelming. At any age. No matter who you are. Man, if it isn't one thing, it's another. If getting older and wiser means anything, it means realizing that *stuff* happens. Now and forever. And it won't end until ya see that wonderful white light.

So you've got to balance it out with fun. Or else. And some of the truest, purest fun out there happens in sports. No question. Thrills, laughs, and camaraderie. The personal triumph(s) of getting better and the simple pleasures of physical exertion.

*I like doing **this** kind of stuff.* I like writing about it. And I like others to get off on it, too.

There it is.

Doug Werner

If you liked this book, we've got more!

All the books in the *Start-Up Sports Series* are written in the conversational, *beginner-friendly* style that the true novice can appreciate. Easy to read. Fun to read. Informative without info overload. Books are available in major bookstores nationwide as well as appropriate surfing, snowboarding, sailing, and skating outlets.

Surfer's Start-Up- A simple intro to surfing. Probably one of the most mystified and romanticized sports on the planet. What to ride and where to ride. How to stand up and angle across the face of a wave. Dealing with the surfing culture and localism. Over 70 photos. Endorsed by Steve Hawk, editor of *Surfer Magazine*. 112 pages. $9.95 retail.

Snowboarder's Start-Up- Another how-to guide for those first fumbling days on the slopes. The fastest growing sport in the world. How to get down the mountain in one piece. How to stop. How to deal with chair lifts. How to traverse and turn. Over 80 photos. Endorsed by Ted Martin, president of the International Snowboard Federation. 128 pages. $9.95 retail.

Continued next page

More Start-Up Books (continued)

Sailor's Start-Up - A beginner's guide that's written in plain english. One of the world's most ancient recreations. How sails work. How to leave the dock and come back into it. How to sail on a reach, upwind and downwind. And catamarans too! Over 100 photos. Endorsed by Chuck Nichols, president of the America's Cup 95. 144 pages. $9.95 retail.

Ordering Start-Up Books

To order books send $9.95 for each book plus $3.00 shipping for the first book and .50 for each additional book. In California add 7% sales tax. Enclose your name and address.

Make checks payable to Tracks Publishing.

Mail check and your address to:

Tracks Publishing
140 Brightwood Avenue
Chula Vista, CA 91910
619-476-7125
Fax 619-476-8173

Thank you!

About the Author

Doug Werner is the creator/author of the highly acclaimed *Start-Up Sports Series*. His books include *Surfer's Start-Up, Snowboarder's Start-Up, Sailor's Start-Up,* and now, *In-Line Skater's Start-Up*. The no-frills, fun-to-read, fun-to-learn instructional series is endorsed by leading publications, manufacturers, organizations, athletes, and coaches in the sporting world. Werner lives in San Diego, California with his wife Kathleen and their two Cairn Terriers, Billy and Lulu.

STREET REVOLUTION

The new Koho Street Revolution is forged from the solid heritage, quality, and feel of Koho professional ice hockey equipment. Koho Street Revolution delivers non-stop utility and the unyielding protection intense players demand. Light, tough, and totally functional, SR goalie, sticks, and protective equipment bring the extreme test of the ice to the street. Join the New Revolution.

STICKS
SHIN GUARDS
ELBOW PADS
GLOVES
GOALIE BLOCKER
CATCHER
PADS
MASK

Koho is a registered trademark, and Street Revolution is a trademark of KHF Sports OY.
Karhu U.S.A. Inc., South Burlington, VT 05403
(802) 864-4519
Karhu Canada, Lachine (Quebec) H8T 3J8
(514) 636-5858